"Animals are such agreeable friends –
they ask no questions, they pass no criticisms."

George Elliot

The Animal Songbook

WISE PUBLICATIONS
part of The Music Sales Group
London / New York / Paris / Sydney / Copenhagen / Madrid / Tokyo / Berlin

Published by
WISE PUBLICATIONS
14-15 Berners Street, London W1T 3LJ,
United Kingdom.

Exclusive Distributors:
MUSIC SALES LIMITED
Distribution Centre, Newmarket Road,
Bury St Edmunds, Suffolk IP33 3YB,
United Kingdom.
MUSIC SALES CORPORATION
257 Park Avenue South, New York, NY 10010,
United States of America.
MUSIC SALES PTY LIMITED
20 Resolution Drive, Caringbah, NSW 2229,
Australia.

Order No. AM993817
ISBN 978-1-84772-578-3
This book © Copyright 2008 Wise Publications,
a division of Music Sales Limited.
Lyrics © Copyright 2008 Dorsey Brothers Limited.
All Rights Reserved.
International Copyright Secured.

Edited by Ann Barkway.
Designed and art directed by Michael Bell Design.
Illustrated by Sonia Canals.
Printed in China.
CD recorded, mixed and mastered by
Jonas Persson.
Backing tracks by Rick Cardinali.
Vocals by Bryn Barton, Sara Cowen, Lois Green,
Jean Squires, Zoe Tankard and Natasha Vakil,
led by Debbie Campbell and Ann Barkway.

www.musicsales.com

ALICE THE CAMEL

Alice the camel has five humps.
Alice the camel has five humps.
Alice the camel has five humps
So go, Alice, go.
Boom, boom, boom.

Alice the camel has four humps.
Alice the camel has four humps.
Alice the camel has four humps
So go, Alice, go.
Boom, boom, boom.

Alice the camel has three humps.
Alice the camel has three humps.
Alice the camel has three humps
So go, Alice, go.
Boom, boom, boom.

Alice the camel has two humps.
Alice the camel has two humps.
Alice the camel has two humps.
So go, Alice, go.
Boom, boom, boom.

Alice the camel has one hump.
Alice the camel has one hump.
Alice the camel has one hump.
So go, Alice, go.
Boom, boom, boom.

Alice the camel has no humps.
Alice the camel has no humps.
Alice the camel has no humps
So Alice is a horse!

ALL THE PRETTY LITTLE HORSES

Hush-you-bye, don't you cry,
Go to sleepy, little baby.
When you wake, you shall have
All the pretty little horses.

Blacks and bays, dapples and greys,
Coach and six-a-little horses.
Hush-you-by, don't you cry,
Go to sleepy, little baby.

THE ANIMAL FAIR

I went to the animal fair,
The birds and the beasts were there.
The big baboon by the light of the moon
Was combing his auburn hair.
The monkey fell out of his bunk, (CLAP)
And slid down the elephant's trunk. (wheee!)
The elephant sneezed and fell on his knees,
And what became of the monkey,
Monkey, monkey, monkey,
Monkey, monkey, monkey, monkey,
Monk? The monk?

The Animal Songbook

BAA BAA BLACK SHEEP

Baa baa black sheep, have you any wool?
Yes sir, yes sir, three bags full.
One for the master, one for the dame,
One for the little boy who lives down the lane.

CHOOK CHOOK

Chook, chook, chook, chook, chook,
"Good morning Mrs Hen.
How many chickens have you got?"
"Madam, I've got ten.
One of them is yellow,
And one of them is brown,
And eight of them are speckle-bred,
The finest in the town."

Chook, chook, chook, chook, chook,
"Good morning Mrs Hen.
How many chickens have you got?"
"Madam, I've got ten.
Two of them are yellow,
And two of them are brown,
And six of them are speckle-bred,
The finest in the town."

Chook, chook, chook, chook, chook,
"Good morning Mrs Hen.
How many chickens have you got?"
"Madam, I've got ten.
Three of them are yellow,
And three of them are brown,
And four of them are speckle-bred,
The finest in the town."

CHOOK CHOOK

16

Chook, chook, chook, chook, chook,
"Good morning Mrs Hen.
How many chickens have you got?"
"Madam, I've got ten.
Four of them are yellow,
And four of them are brown,
And two of them are speckle-bred,
The finest in the town."

Chook, chook, chook, chook, chook,
"Good morning Mrs Hen.
How many chickens have you got?"
"Madam, I've got ten.
Five of them are yellow,
And five of them are brown,
And none of them are speckle-bred,
The finest in the town."

BINGO

There was a farmer, had a dog,
And Bingo was his name-o.
B-I-N-G-O!
B-I-N-G-O!
B-I-N-G-O!
And Bingo was his name-o.

DING DONG BELL

Ding dong bell! Pussy's in the well.
Who put her in? Little Tommy Green.
Who pulled her out? Little Tommy Stout.
What a naughty boy was that
To drown poor pussy cat,
Who ne'er did any harm,
But killed all the mice in his father's barn.

DADDY FOX

Daddy Fox went out on a chilly night,
With a ling-tong dilly-dong kye-ro-me;
And he prayed for the moon to give him light,
With a ling-tong dilly-dong kye-ro-me.

CHORUS...
Hey! Fa-la-le, fa-la-la,
Fa-la-lay-ro.
Hey! Fa-la-lay-ro, lay-ro-lee.
Up jumps John,
Ringing on his bell,
With a ling-tong dilly-dong kye-ro-me.

The Animal Songbook

23

Well, he ran till he came to a great big pen,
With a ling-tong dilly-dong kye-ro-me;
And the ducks and the geese were kept therein,
With a ling-tong dilly-dong kye-ro-me.

CHORUS

He grabbed the grey goose by the neck,
With a ling-tong dilly-dong kye-ro-me;
And up with the little ones over his back,
With a ling-tong dilly-dong kye-ro-me.

CHORUS

Old Mother Flipper-Flopper jumped out of bed,
With a ling-tong dilly-dong kye-ro-me;
Out of the window she stuck her little head,
With a ling-tong dilly-dong kye-ro-me.

CHORUS

DADDY FOX

24

John, he ran to the top of the hill,
With a ling-tong dilly-dong kye-ro-me;
And he blew his little horn both loud and shrill,
With a ling-tong dilly-dong kye-ro-me.

CHORUS

The fox, he ran to his cosy den,
With a ling-tong dilly-dong kye-ro-me;
And there were the little ones, eight, nine, ten,
With a ling-tong dilly-dong kye-ro-me.

CHORUS

Then the fox and his wife, without any strife,
With a ling-tong dilly-dong kye-ro-me;
They cut up the goose with a carving knife,
With a ling-tong dilly-dong kye-ro-me.

CHORUS

EENSY WEENSY SPIDER

The eensy weensy spider went up the water spout.
Down came the rain and washed the spider out.
Out came the sun and dried up all the rain.
Now the eensy weensy spider went up the spout again.

POP GOES THE WEASEL

Half a pound of two-penny rice,
Half a pound of treacle,
That's the way the money goes,
Pop goes the weasel.

FIVE LITTLE DUCKS

TRACK 11

Five little ducks went swimming one day,
Over the hills and far away.
The mother duck said,
"Quack, quack, quack, quack"
And only four little ducks came back.

The Animal Songbook

31

Four little ducks went swimming one day,
Over the hills and far away.
The mother duck said,
    "Quack, quack, quack, quack"
And only three little ducks came back.

Three little ducks went swimming one day,
Over the hills and far away.
The mother duck said,
    "Quack, quack, quack, quack"
And only two little ducks came back.

Two little ducks went swimming one day,
Over the hills and far away.
The mother duck said,
    "Quack, quack, quack, quack"
And only one little duck came back.

FIVE LITTLE DUCKS

One little duck went swimming one day,
Over the hills and far away.
The mother duck said,
   "Quack, quack, quack, quack"
And five little ducks came swimming right back.

OLD MACDONALD

Old MacDonald had a farm,
Ee-eye, ee-eye, oh!
And on that farm he had some chicks,
Ee-eye, ee-eye, oh!
With a chick-chick here and a chick-chick there,
Here a chick, there a chick,
    everywhere a chick-chick.
Old MacDonald had a farm,
Ee-eye, ee-eye, oh!

Old MacDonald had a farm,
Ee-eye, ee-eye, oh!
And on that farm he had some ducks,
Ee-eye, ee-eye, oh!
With a quack-quack here and a quack-quack there,
Here a quack, there a quack,
everywhere a quack-quack.
Chick-chick here and a chick-chick there,
Here a chick, there a chick,
everywhere a chick-chick.
Old MacDonald had a farm,
Ee-eye, ee-eye, oh!

...and on that farm he had some cows...
With a moo-moo here and a moo-moo there,
Here a moo, there a moo, everywhere a moo-moo,
Quack-quack here and a quack-quack there...
Chick-chick here and a chick-chick there...

...and on that farm he had some pigs...
With an oink-oink here and an oink-oink there,
Here an oink, there and oink,
    everywhere and oink-oink,
Moo-moo here...
Quack-quack here...
Chick-chick here...

...and on that farm he had some sheep...
With a baa-baa here and a baa-baa there...
Oink-oink here...
Moo-moo here...
Quack-quack here...
Chick-chick here...

FIVE LITTLE SPECKLED FROGS

Five little speckled frogs
Sat on a speckled log,
Eating some most delicious bugs,
Yum! Yum!
One jumped into the pool,
Where it was nice and cool,
Now there are just four speckled frogs,
Glub! Glub!

Four little speckled frogs
Sat on a speckled log,
Eating some most delicious bugs,
Yum! Yum!
One jumped into the pool,
Where it was nice and cool,
Now there are just three speckled frogs,
Glub! Glub!

Three little speckled frogs
Sat on a speckled log,
Eating some most delicious bugs,
Yum! Yum!
One jumped into the pool,
Where it was nice and cool,
Now there are just two speckled frogs,
Glub! Glub!

Two little speckled frogs
Sat on a speckled log,
Eating some most delicious bugs,
Yum! Yum!
One jumped into the pool,
Where it was nice and cool,
Now there is just one speckled frog,
Glub! Glub!

One little speckled frog
Sat on a speckled log,
Eating some most delicious bugs,
Yum! Yum!
One jumped into the pool,
Where it was nice and cool,
Now there are no more speckled frogs,
Glub! Glub!

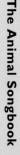

I KNOW AN OLD LADY WHO SWALLOWED A FLY

I know an old lady who swallowed a fly,
I don't know why she swallowed a fly,
Perhaps she'll die!

I know an old lady who swallowed a spider
That wriggled and jiggled and tickled inside her.
She swallowed the spider to catch the fly,
I don't know why she swallowed a fly,
Perhaps she'll die!

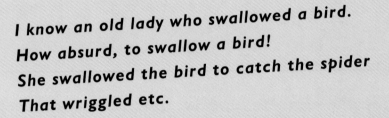

I know an old lady who swallowed a bird.
How absurd, to swallow a bird!
She swallowed the bird to catch the spider
That wriggled etc.

I know an old lady who swallowed a cat,
Just fancy that, she swallowed a cat!
She swallowed the cat to catch the bird,
She swallowed the bird to catch the spider etc.

I know an old lady who swallowed a dog,
What a hog, to swallow a dog!
She swallowed the dog to catch the cat,
She swallowed the cat to catch the bird, etc.

I know an old lady who swallowed a goat.
She just opened her throat and swallowed a goat!
She swallowed the goat to catch the dog,
She swallowed the dog to catch the cat, etc.

I know an old lady who swallowed a cow.
I don't know HOW she swallowed a cow.
She swallowed the cow to catch the goat,
She swallowed the goat to catch the dog, etc.

GOOSEY GOOSEY GANDER

Goosey, goosey, gander, whither shall I wander?
Upstairs and downstairs and in my lady's chamber.
There I met an old man who would not
   say his prayers.
So I took him by the left leg and
   threw him down the stairs.

HARK, HARK, THE DOGS DO BARK

TRACK 16

Hark, hark, the dogs do bark,
Beggars are coming to town.
Some in Jags and some in rags
And some in velvet gowns.

LITTLE BIRD

Little bird, little bird,
Go through my window,
Little bird, little bird,
Go through my window,
Little bird, little bird,
Go through my window,
And buy molasses candy.

CHORUS...
Go through my window,
My sugar lump,
Go through my window,
My sugar lump,
And buy molasses candy.

The Animal Songbook

51

Blue bird, blue bird,
Fly through my window,
Blue bird, blue bird,
Fly through my window,
Blue bird, blue bird,
Fly through my window,
And buy molasses candy.

LITTLE BIRD

CHORUS...

Fly through my window,

My little bird,

Fly through my window,

My little bird,

And buy molasses candy.

LADYBIRD, LADYBIRD

Ladybird, ladybird, fly away home,
Your house is on fire and your children are gone.

OLD BLUE

Had an old dog and his name was Blue.
Had an old dog and his name was Blue.
Had an old dog and his name was Blue.
Bet you five dollars was a good dog, too.

Every night just about dark (3 TIMES)
Blue goes out and begins to bark.

CHORUS...
Bye bye Blue.
You're a good dog, you.

Everything just in a rush (3 TIMES)
He treed a possum in a white-oak bush.

CHORUS

Possum walked out to the end of a limb (3 TIMES)
Blue set down and talked to him.

CHORUS

Blue got sick and very sick (3 TIMES)
Sent for the doctor to come here quick.

CHORUS

Doctor come and he come in a run (3 TIMES)
Says, "Old Blue, your hunting's done".

CHORUS

OLD BLUE

58

Blue he died and died so hard
   (3 TIMES)
Scratched little holes all
   around the yard.

CHORUS

Laid him out in a shady place (3 TIMES)
Covered him o'er with a possum's face.

CHORUS

When I get to heaven I'll tell you what I'll do (3 TIMES)
I'll take my horn and blow for Blue.

CHORUS

TRACK 20

OH WHERE HAS MY LITTLE DOG GONE?

The Animal Songbook

Oh where, oh where has my little dog gone?
Oh where, oh where, can he be?
With his ears cut short and his tail cut long,
Oh where, oh where can he be?

RIDE A COCK HORSE

Ride a cock horse to Banbury cross,
To see a fine lady ride on a white horse.
Rings on her fingers and bells on her toes
And she shall have music wherever she goes.

OLD HOGAN'S GOAT

(second voice in brackets)

There was a man...
         (there was a man)

Now please take note...
         (now please take note)

There was a man...
         (there was a man)

Who had a goat...
         (who had a goat)

He loved that goat...
         (he loved that goat)

Indeed he did...
         (indeed he did)

He loved that goat...
         (he loved that goat)

Just like a kid...
         (just like a kid)

One day that goat...
                    (one day that goat)

Was feeling fine...
                    (was feeling fine)

Ate three red shirts...
                    (ate three red shirts)

From off the line...
                    (from off the line)

The old man grabbed...
                    (the old man grabbed)

Her by the back...
                    (her by the back)

And tied her to...
                    (and tied her to)

The railway track...
                    (the railway track)

OLD HOGAN'S GOAT

Now when the train...
            (now when the train)

Came into sight...
            (came into sight)

The goat grew pale...
            (the goat grew pale)

And grey with fright...
            (and grey with fright)

She struggled hard...
            (she struggled hard)

And then again...
            (and then again)

Coughed up the shirts...
            (coughed up the shirts)

And flagged the train...
            (and flagged the train)

The Animal Songbook

TRACK 2 3

TWO LITTLE DICKIE BIRDS

Two little dickie birds, sitting on a wall;
One named Peter, one named Paul.
Fly away, Peter! Fly away, Paul!
Come back, Peter! Come Back, Paul!

The Animal Songbook

THE ANTS
CAME MARCHING

The ants came marching one by one;
   Hurrah! Hurrah!
The ants came marching one by one;
   Hurrah! Hurrah!
The ants came marching one by one,
The little one stopped to suck his thumb,
And they all go marching down around the town.
(Boom, boom, boom.)

The ants came marching two by two;
   Hurrah! Hurrah!
The ants came marching two by two;
   Hurrah! Hurrah!
The ants came marching two by two,
The little one stopped to tie his shoe,
And they all go marching down around the town.
(Boom, boom, boom.)

The Animal Songbook

71

The ants came marching three by three;
    Hurrah! Hurrah!
The ants came marching three by three;
    Hurrah! Hurrah!
The ants came marching three by three,
The little one stopped to climb a tree,
And they all go marching down around the town.
(Boom, boom, boom.)

The ants came marching four by four...
The little one stopped to shut the door...

The ants came marching five by five...
The little one stopped to take a dive...

THE ANTS CAME MARCHING

The ants came marching six by six...
The little one stopped to pick up sticks...

The ants came marching seven by seven...
The little one stopped to go to heaven...

The ants came marching eight by eight...
The little one stopped to shut the gate...

The ants came marching nine by nine...
The little one stopped to scratch his spine...

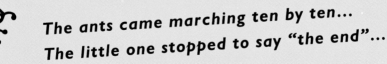

The ants came marching ten by ten...
The little one stopped to say "the end"...

ONE ELEPHANT

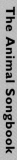

TRACK 25

One elephant went out to play
Upon a spider's web one day.
He found it such enormous fun
That he called for another elephant to come.

MARY HAD A LITTLE LAMB

Mary had a little lamb,
Little lamb, little lamb,
Mary had a little lamb,
Its fleece as white as snow.

And ev'rywhere that Mary went,
Mary went, Mary went,
Ev'rywhere that Mary went,
The lamb was sure to go.

The Animal Songbook

77

It followed her to school one day,
School one day, school one day.
It followed her to school one day,
Which was against the rules.

It made the children laugh and play,
Laugh and play, laugh and play.
It made the children laugh and play,
To see a lamb at school.

And so the teacher turned it out,
Turned it out, turned it out.
And so the teacher turned it out,
But still it lingered near.

MARY HAD A LITTLE LAMB

And waited patiently about,
'Ly about, 'ly about.
And waited patiently about,
Till Mary did appear.

Why does the lamb love Mary so?
Mary so, Mary so?
Why does the lamb love Mary so?
The eager children cry.

Why, Mary loves the lamb, you know,
Lamb, you know, lamb, you know.
Why, Mary loves the lamb, you know,
The teacher did reply.

THE BARNYARD SONG

I had a cat, and the cat pleased me,
I fed my cat under yonder tree;
Cat goes fiddle dee dee.

I had a hen, and the hen pleased me,
I fed my hen under yonder tree;
Hen goes chimmy chuck, chimmy chuck,
Cat goes fiddle dee dee.

I had a duck, etc.
...Duck goes quack, quack, quack, quack,
Hen goes chimmy chuck, chimmy chuck,
Cat goes fiddle dee dee.

I had a pig, etc.
...Pig goes oink, oink, oink, oink,
Duck goes quack, quack, quack, quack,
Hen goes chimmy chuck, chimmy chuck,
Cat goes fiddle dee dee.

I had a sheep, etc.
...Sheep goes *baaa, baaa, baaa, baaa,*
Pig goes *oink, oink, oink, oink,*
Duck goes *quack, quack, quack, quack,*
Hen goes *chimmy chuck, chimmy chuck,*
Cat goes *fiddle dee dee.*

    I had a turkey, etc.
    ...Turkey goes *gibble-gobble, gibble-gobble,*
    Sheep goes *baaa, baaa, baaa, baaa,*
    Pig goes *oink, oink, oink, oink,*
    Duck goes *quack, quack, quack, quack,*
    Hen goes *chimmy chuck, chimmy chuck,*
    Cat goes *fiddle dee dee.*

ONE, TWO, THREE, FOUR, FIVE

One, two, three, four, five,
Once I caught a fish alive.
Six, seven, eight, nine, ten,
Then I let it go again.

Why did you let it go?
Because it bit my finger so.
Which finger did it bite?
This little finger on the right.

THE BEAR WENT OVER THE MOUNTAIN

Oh, the bear went over the mountain,
The bear went over the mountain,
The bear went over the mountain to
   see what he could see.
To see what he could see,
To see what he could see.
Oh, the bear went over the mountain to
   see what he could see.

Oh, he saw another mountain,
He saw another mountain,
He saw another mountain and that's
   what he could see.
And that's what he could see,
And that's what he could see,
Oh, he saw another mountain and that's
   what he could see.

TRACK 30

TEN LITTLE PIGS

Ten little pigs went to market,
One of them fell down,
One of them he ran away,
How many got to town?
Eight!

Eight little pigs went to market,
One of them fell down,
One of them he ran away,
How many got to town?
Six!

Six little pigs went to market,
One of them fell down,
One of them he ran away,
How many got to town?
Four!

TEN LITTLE PIGS

90

Four little pigs went to market,
One of them fell down,
One of them he ran away,
How many got to town?
Two!

Two little pigs went to market,
One of them fell down,
One of them he ran away,
How many got to town?
None!

TRACK 31

PUSSY CAT

"Pussy cat, pussy cat, where have you been?"
"I've been to London to see the new Queen."
"Pussy cat, pussy cat, what did you there?"
"I caught a little mouse under her chair."

The Animal Songbook

THE OWL AND THE PUSSYCAT

The Owl and the Pussy-Cat went to sea
In a beautiful pea-green boat;
They took some honey, and plenty of money
Wrapped up in a five-pound note.
The Owl looked up to the stars above,
And sang to a small guitar:
"O lovely Pussy! O Pussy, my love,
What a beautiful Pussy you are,
You are,
You are,
What a beautiful Pussy you are!"

Pussy said to the Owl: "You elegant fowl,
How charmingly sweet you sing!
Oh, let us be married; too long we have tarried;
But what shall we do for a ring?"
They sailed away for a year and a day
To the land where the bong tree grows;
And there in the woods, a piggy-wig stood
With a ring at the end of his nose,

His nose,
His nose,
With a ring at the end of his nose.

"Dear Pig, are you willing to sell for one shilling
Your ring?" Said the piggy, "I will."
So they took it away, and were married next day
By the turkey who lives on the hill.
They dined on mince and slices of quince,
Which they ate with a runcible spoon,
And hand in hand on the edge of the sand,
They danced by the light of the moon,
The moon,
The moon,
They danced by the light of the moon.

TRACK 33

TWO LITTLE CHICKENS

Two little chickens looking for some more,
Along came another two and they make four.
Run to the haystack, run to the pen,
Run little chickens, back to Mother Hen.

Four little chickens getting in a fix,
Along came another two and they make six.
Run to the haystack, run to the pen,
Run little chickens, back to Mother Hen.

Six little chickens perching on a gate,
Along came another two and they make eight.
Run to the haystack, run to the pen,
Run little chickens, back to Mother Hen.

Eight little chickens run to Mother Hen,
Along came another two and they make ten.
Run to the haystack, run to the pen,
Run little chickens, back to Mother Hen.

WHY DOESN'T MY GOOSE?

Why doesn't my goose lay as much as thy goose
When I paid for my goose twice as much as thine?

THREE LITTLE KITTENS

Once three little kittens they lost their mittens,
And they began to cry:
"Oh, mother dear, we sadly fear
Our mittens we have lost!"
"What? Lost your mittens! You naughty kittens!
Then you shall have no pie."
"Meow, meow, meow, meow!"

The three little kittens, they found their mittens,
And they began to cry:
"Oh, mother dear, see here, see here!
Our mittens we have found!"
"What? Found your mittens? You darling kittens!
Then you shall have some pie!"
"Meow, meow, meow, meow!"

The three little kittens put on their mittens,
And soon ate up their pie,
"Oh, mother dear, we greatly fear,
Our mittens we have soiled!"
"What? Soiled your mittens? You naughty kittens!"
Then they began to sigh,
"Meow, meow, meow, meow!"

The three little kittens, they washed their mittens,
And hung them up to dry.
"Oh, mother dear, look here, look here!
Our mittens we have washed!"
"What? Washed your mittens? You darling kittens!
But I smell a rat close by.
Hush, hush, hush, hush."

TRACK 36

THIS LITTLE PIG
WENT TO MARKET

This little pig went to market,
   this little pig stayed at home.
This little pig had roast beef,
   this little pig had none,
And this little pig cried,
   "we-we, we-we, we," all the way home.

The Animal Songbook

FIELD MICE

Down in the meadow where the long grass grows,
There were five little field mice washing their clothes,
With a rub-a-dub here and a rub-a-dub there,
That's the way the field mice wash their clothes.

CHORUS...
With a squeak, squeak, squeak, boogie woogie!
Squeak, squeak, squeak, boogie woogie!
Squeak, squeak, squeak, boogie woogie!
That's the way the field mice wash their clothes.

Down in the meadow where the long grass grows,
There were four little field mice washing their clothes,
With a rub-a-dub here and a rub-a-dub there,
That's the way the field mice wash their clothes.

The Animal Songbook

CHORUS

Down in the meadow where the long grass grows,
There were three little field mice washing their clothes,
With a rub-a-dub here and a rub-a-dub there,
That's the way the field mice wash their clothes.

CHORUS

Down in the meadow where the long grass grows,
There were two little field mice washing their clothes,
With a rub-a-dub here and a rub-a-dub there,
That's the way the field mice wash their clothes.

CHORUS

Down in the meadow where the long grass grows,
There was one little field mouse washing his clothes,
With a rub-a-dub here and a rub-a-dub there,
That's the way the field mouse washes his clothes.

CHORUS

FIELD MICE